THE NERVOUS SYSTEM

BY JOELLE RILEY

LERNER PUBLICATIONS COMPANY • MINNEAPOLIS

For Teri, my wise friend

The photographs in this book are used with the permission of: © Stockbyte, pp. 5, 33, 43; © Jim Cartier/Photo Researchers, Inc., p. 6; © Bachmann/Photo Researchers, Inc., p. 7; © Diane M. Meyer, pp. 8, 29, 37, 41; © Wolfgang Schmidt/Peter Arnold, Inc., p. 9; © Lester Lefkowitz/CORBIS, p. 11; © David M. Phillips/ Photo Researchers, Inc., p. 12; © Ed Reschke/ Peter Arnold, Inc., p. 14; © SPL/Photo Researchers, Inc., p. 15; © Ralph C. Eagle, Jr./Photo Researchers, Inc., p. 16; © Don W. Fawcett/Photo Researchers, Inc., p. 17; © Sercomi/Photo Researchers, Inc., p. 18; Royalty-Free/CORBIS, pp. 19, 48 (top); © Science Photo Library/ Photo Researchers, Inc., p. 20; © Astrid & Hanns-Frieder Michler/Photo Researchers, Inc., p. 22; © Scott Camazine & Sue Trainor/Photo Researchers, Inc., p. 23; Photodisc Royalty Free by Getty Images, pp. 24, 34; © D. Roberts/Photo Researchers, Inc., p. 25; © CNRI/Photo Researchers, Inc., p. 27; © Damien Lovegrove/Photo Researchers, Inc., p. 28; © Manfred Kage/Peter Arnold, Inc., p. 30; © Geoff Tompkinson/ Photo Researchers, Inc., p. 31; © Volker Steger/Peter Arnold, Inc., p. 32; © Eye of Science/Photo Researchers, Inc., p. 35; © Todd Strand/Independent Picture Service, p. 36; © SPL/Photo Researchers, Inc., p. 38; © Nana Twumasi/Independent Picture Service, p. 40; Eyewire by Getty Images, p. 42; © The Photo Works/Photo Researchers, Inc., p. 46; © Lawrence Migdale/Photo Researchers, Inc., p. 47; © Jeff Greenberg/Peter Arnold, Inc., p. 48 (bottom).

Front Cover: © BSIP Agency/Index Stock Imagery.

Illustrations courtesy of Laura Westlund, pp. 4, 10, 13, 21, 26, 39

Text copyright © 2005 by Lerner Publications Company

Lerner Publications Company
A division of Lerner Publishing Group
241 First Avenue North
Minneapolis, MN 55401 U.S.A.

Website address: www.lernerbooks.com

Library of Congress Cataloging-in-Publication Data

Riley, Joelle.
    The nervous system / by Joelle Riley.
       p.   cm. — (Early bird body systems)
    Includes index.
    ISBN: 0–8225–1249–1 (lib. bdg. : alk. paper)
    1. Nervous system—Juvenile literature. I. Title. II. Series.
QP361.5.R53 2005
612.8—dc22   2004002613

Manufactured in the United States of America
1 2 3 4 5 6 – JR – 10 09 08 07 06 05

CONTENTS

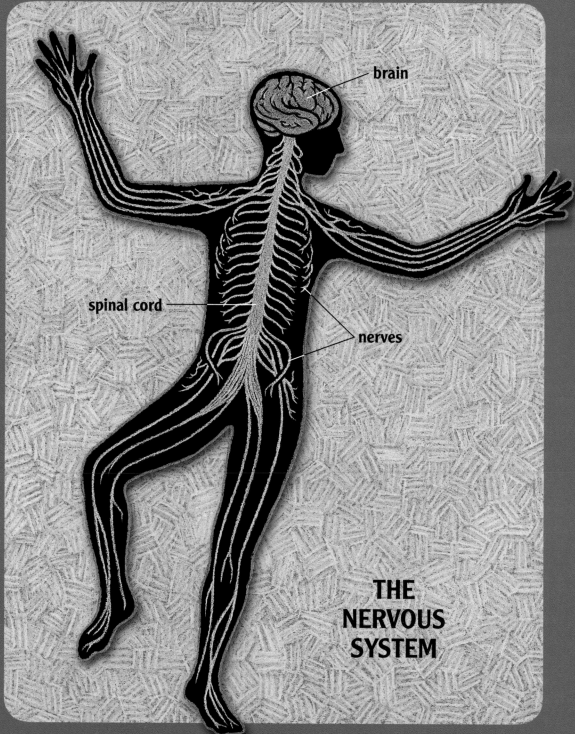

brain

spinal cord

nerves

THE NERVOUS SYSTEM

BE A WORD DETECTIVE

Can you find these words as you read about the nervous system? Be a detective and try to figure out what they mean. You can turn to the glossary on page 46 for help.

brain	cortex	reflexes
brain stem	nerves	skull
cerebellum	organs	spinal cord
cerebrum	receptors	

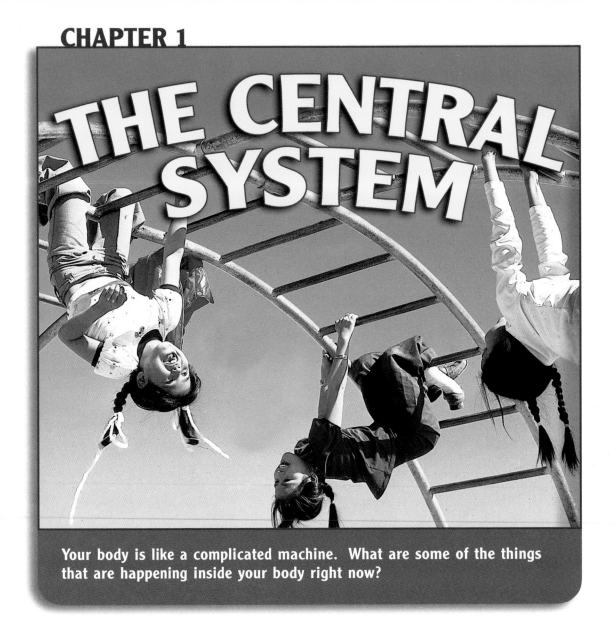

CHAPTER 1

THE CENTRAL SYSTEM

Your body is like a complicated machine. What are some of the things that are happening inside your body right now?

Your body has many systems. A system is a way of doing things. Your body's systems help it do the things it needs to do to stay alive.

Your muscles and bones help you move. Your heart pumps blood through your body. Your lungs bring in air. And your stomach breaks down the food you eat. But what keeps all of these systems working?

Your body's systems help you to do things like playing games.

Your nervous system controls all of the other systems. It keeps track of everything that happens in your body. It tells your other systems what to do. Without your nervous system, none of your other systems could do their jobs.

Your nervous system keeps all your other systems working. It also helps you think.

Your nervous system tells your muscles how to move.

But your nervous system does much more than just control your other systems. Your nervous system helps you dance. It helps you solve puzzles. It helps you laugh. It helps you remember the names of your friends. It helps you see flowers and hear music. It even helps you dream.

THE BRAIN TELLS MUSCLES WHAT TO DO

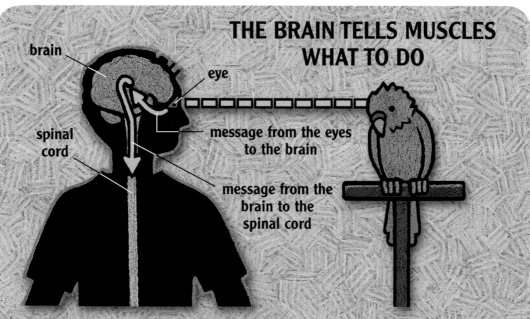

brain

eye

spinal cord

message from the eyes to the brain

message from the brain to the spinal cord

When you see something interesting, your eyes send a message to your brain. Your brain decides what to do and sends a message to your spinal cord.

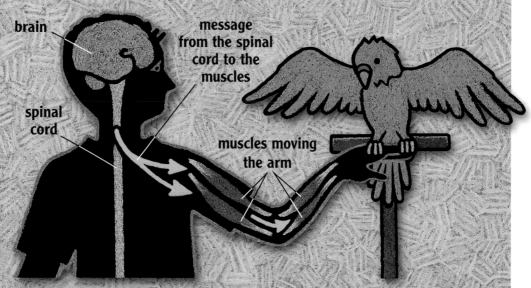

brain

message from the spinal cord to the muscles

spinal cord

muscles moving the arm

Your spinal cord passes the message on to your muscles. The message tells your muscles what to do.

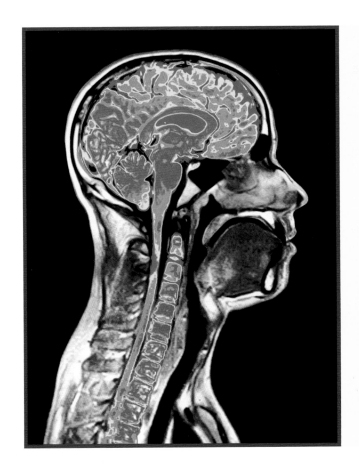

This picture shows the inside of a person's head and neck. The colored parts of the picture show the brain and the spinal cord.

Your nervous system is made up of your nerves, your spinal cord, and your brain. Nerves carry messages to and from all parts of your body. Your spinal cord connects your nerves to your brain. Your brain thinks. It keeps track of everything that happens in your body. It tells the other body systems what to do.

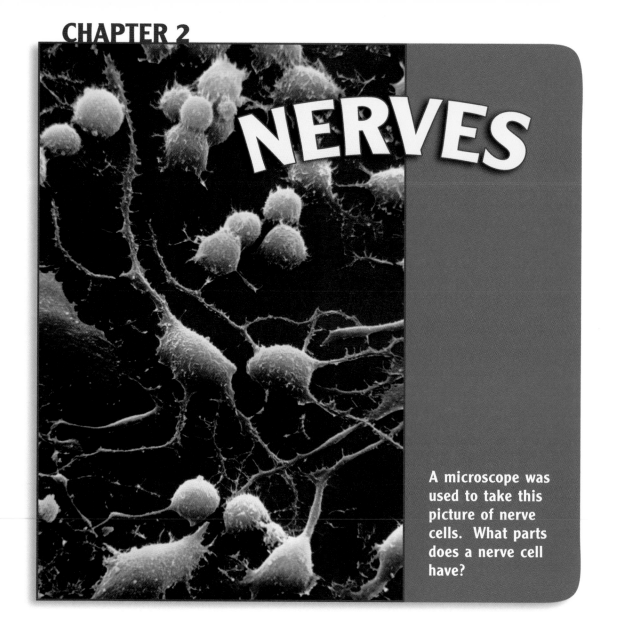

CHAPTER 2

NERVES

A microscope was used to take this picture of nerve cells. What parts does a nerve cell have?

Your nerves are made up of special cells called nerve cells. A nerve cell's job is to collect messages and pass them on.

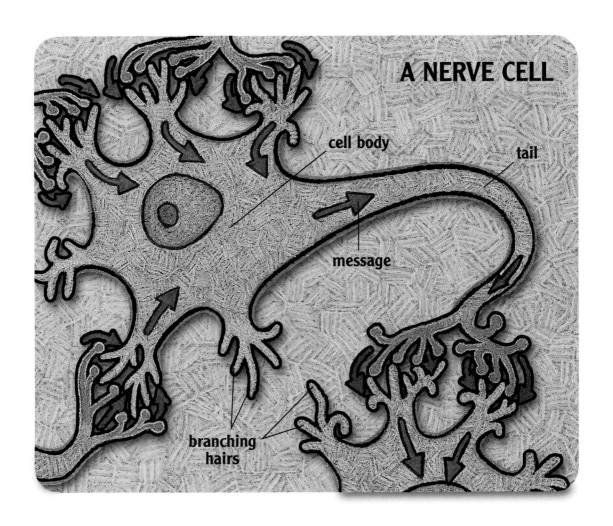

A NERVE CELL

cell body

tail

message

branching hairs

Each nerve cell has a body, a tail, and branching parts that look like hairs. A nerve cell's hairs collect a message. The message travels through the hairs. It goes through the cell's body. Then it moves down the tail. The tail passes the message to the hairs on another nerve cell.

Nerve cells are tiny. You would need a microscope to see one. But many nerve cells are bundled together to make nerves. Nerves are big enough to be seen without a microscope.

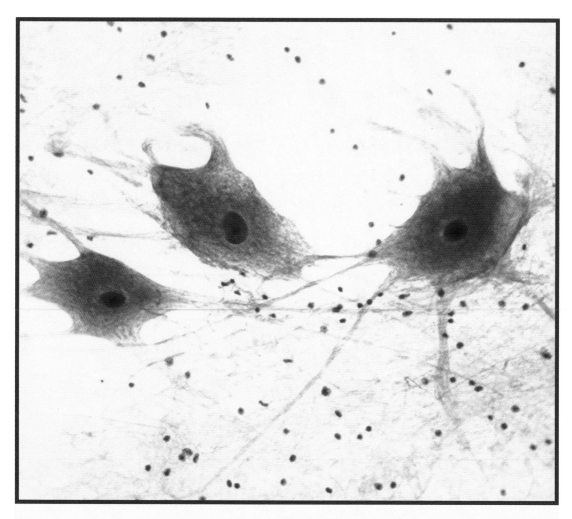

This picture shows three nerve cells up close.

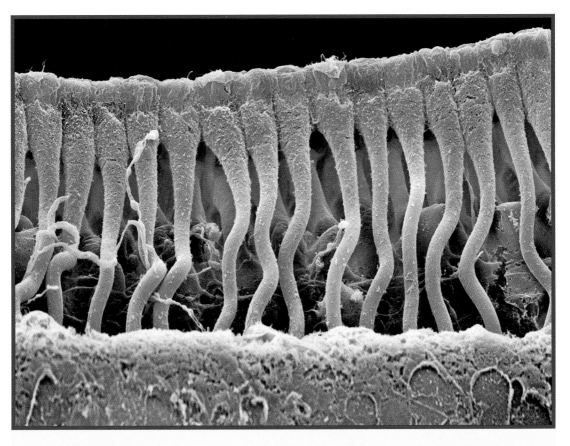

The cells in this picture are deep inside a person's ear. Nerve cells in this part of your ear collect information about the sounds you hear.

Some nerve cells collect messages from your skin or from other parts of your body. These nerve cells are called receptors (rih-SEHP-turz). Receptors collect information from the world and from your body.

Receptors in your skin, ears, eyes, nose, and tongue collect messages from the world around you. Other receptors collect messages from inside your body. Nerve cells pass these messages to your spinal cord or your brain.

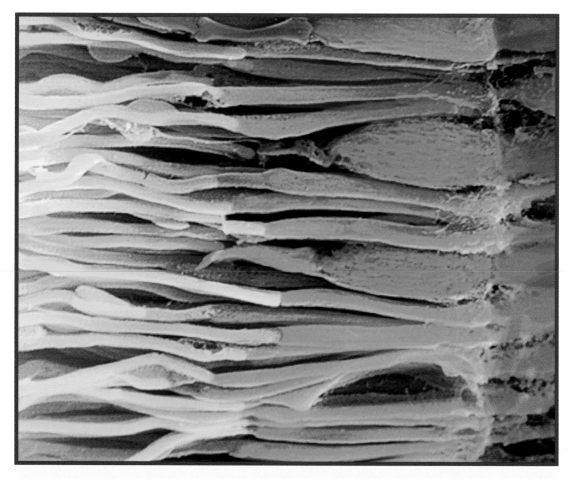

Special cells inside the eye collect information about things that you see.

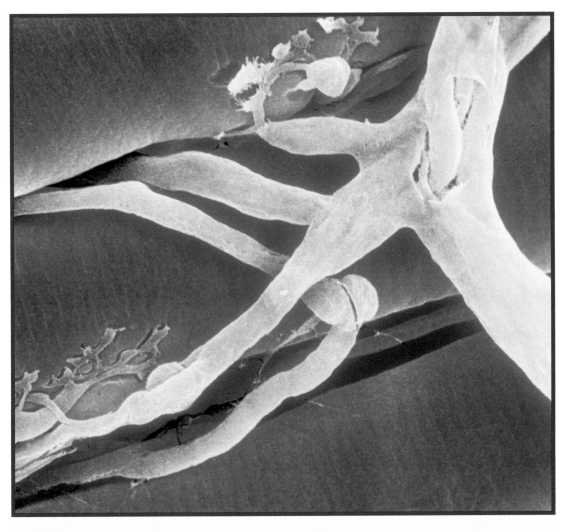

This picture shows a nerve that carries messages to muscle cells.

Other nerve cells collect messages from your brain. They carry these messages to your muscles or to other parts of your body.

A nerve is like a telephone cable that is made up of many different wires. A telephone cable can send many calls at once, because each wire can send one call. A nerve can send many messages at once too. Each nerve cell can send a different message.

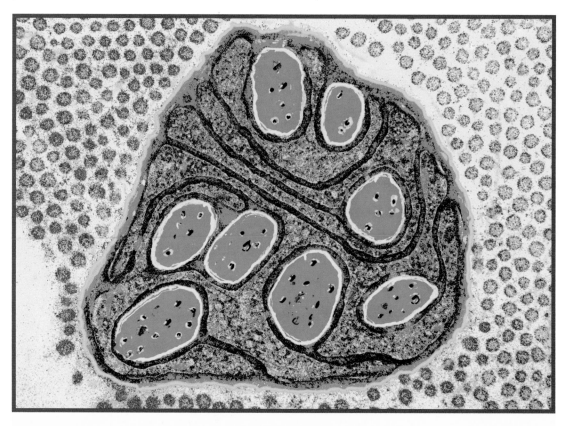

Each nerve is made of bundles of nerve cells. This picture shows the inside of a nerve.

Nerves send messages very quickly. They help you to move fast when you play soccer.

Nerves are in every part of your body. Messages travel very quickly through your nerves. A message can travel from your brain to your foot faster than you can blink your eyes!

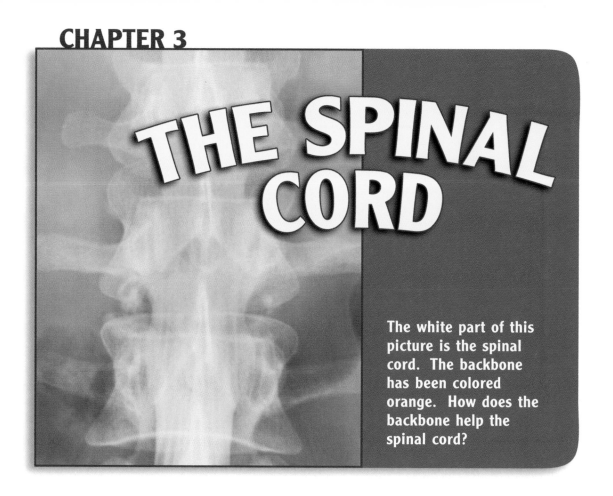

CHAPTER 3

THE SPINAL CORD

The white part of this picture is the spinal cord. The backbone has been colored orange. How does the backbone help the spinal cord?

Your spinal cord is a thick bundle of nerves. It looks like a white rope. The spinal cord got its name from the spine. Another name for the spine is the backbone. Your spinal cord fits through holes in your backbone. The hard backbone keeps your spinal cord from being hurt.

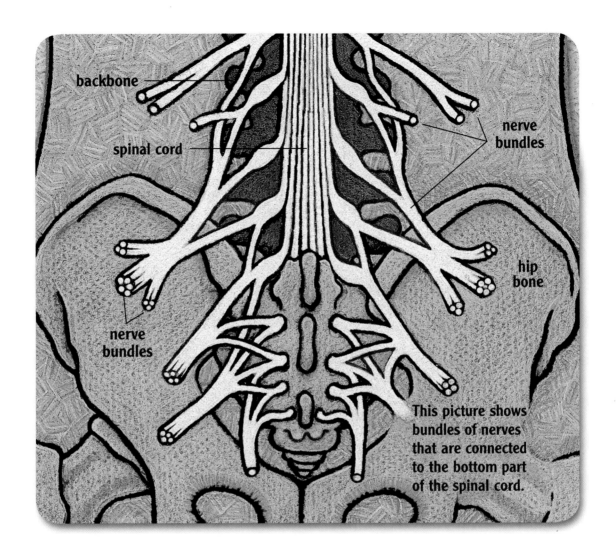

Labels in the image: backbone, spinal cord, nerve bundles, nerve bundles, hip bone

This picture shows bundles of nerves that are connected to the bottom part of the spinal cord.

Bundles of nerves from all over your body meet up with the spinal cord. Some of the nerves collect messages from your spinal cord. They pass these messages to other parts of your body.

Other nerves pass messages to the spinal cord. Your spinal cord sends these messages on to your brain.

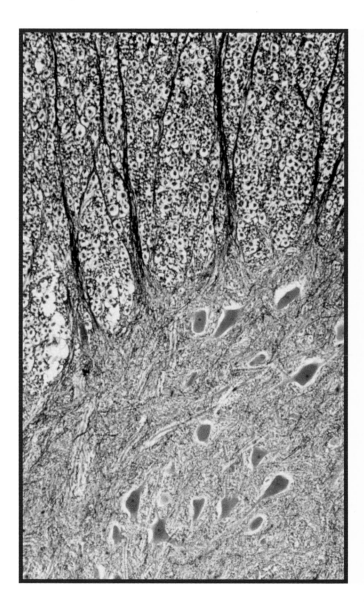

This picture shows hundreds of nerve cells inside the spinal cord.

CHAPTER 4

THE BRAIN

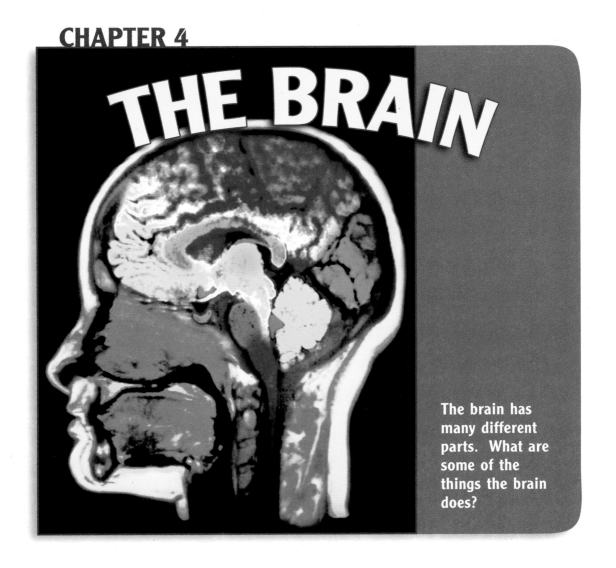

The brain has many different parts. What are some of the things the brain does?

Your brain is the part of your body that makes you who you are. It helps you speak. And it helps you understand what others are saying. It remembers the things you have done, seen, and learned.

Your brain makes you feel happy or sad. It decides what your favorite colors and foods are. It helps you learn to ride a bike. It helps you do a cartwheel. And it keeps the rest of your body working the way it is supposed to.

Your brain helps all the parts of your body work together.

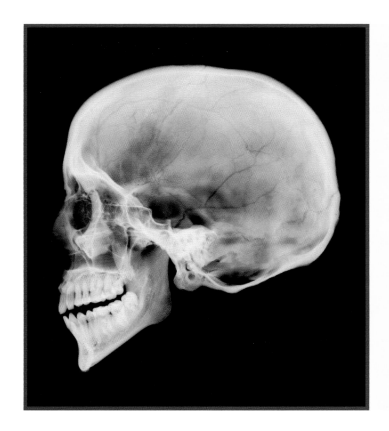

The round part of the skull protects the brain. It is made up of eight flat bones that fit together like puzzle pieces.

Your brain is very soft. But your skull protects your brain. Your skull is made up of hard bones. The bones fit together tightly. They keep your brain from being hurt, even if you fall and bump your head.

Inside your skull, your brain floats in clear liquid. The liquid keeps your brain from banging against your skull and being hurt.

Your brain has three main parts. The three parts are called the brain stem, the cerebellum (SAIR-uh-BEHL-uhm), and the cerebrum (suh-REE-bruhm). Each part has important jobs to do.

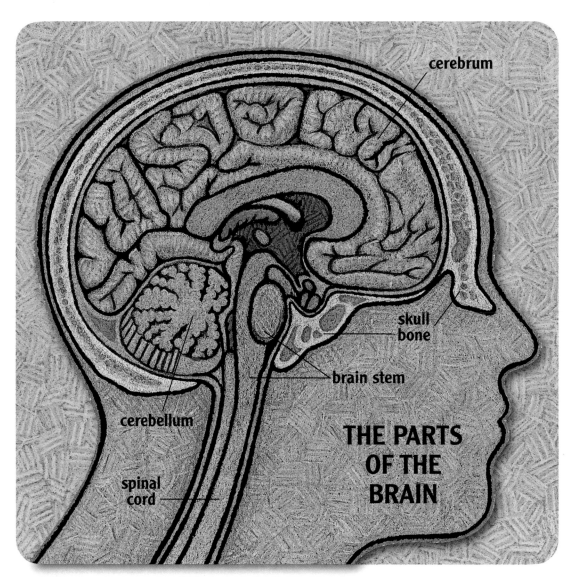

cerebrum

skull bone

brain stem

cerebellum

spinal cord

THE PARTS OF THE BRAIN

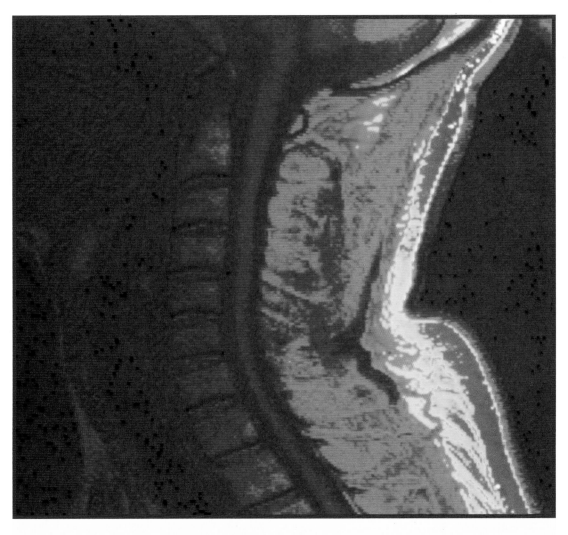

The brain stem is attached to the spinal cord at the top of the neck.

Your brain stem passes messages between your brain and your spinal cord. It also controls the movement of your head and neck.

Your brain stem also controls the things that your body does on its own. It keeps your heart beating and your lungs breathing. It controls how the food you eat is broken down. It controls sleeping and dreaming. It also controls swallowing, vomiting, sneezing, coughing, and hiccuping!

Your brain stem controls sneezing.

Your cerebellum helps you keep your balance when you ride a skateboard.

Your cerebellum controls how you move. It helps you keep your balance. It also stores memories of how to do things, like eating with a fork or riding a skateboard.

Your cerebrum is the biggest part of your brain. The outside layer of the cerebrum is called the cortex. The cortex has deep wrinkles. The wrinkles help the cortex to take up less space. It's like crumpling a big piece of paper into a tiny ball to make the paper smaller.

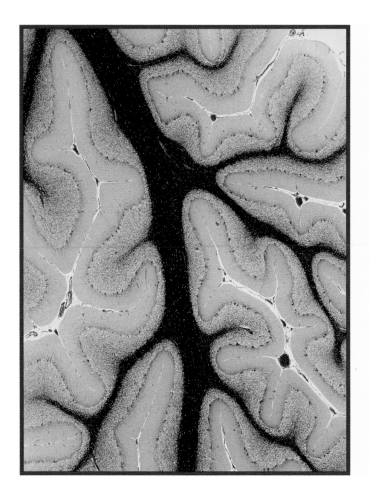

This picture shows the inside of the cerebellum.

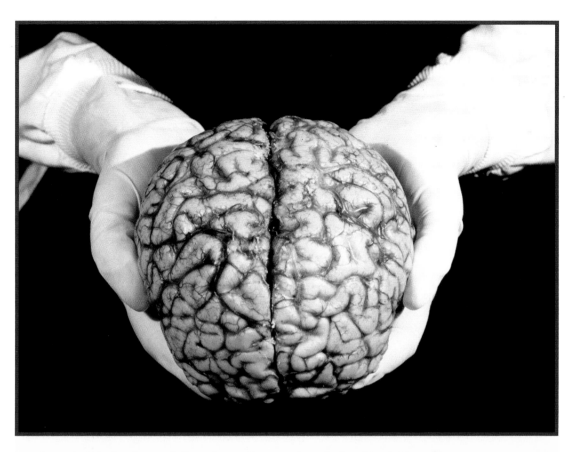

An adult's brain weighs about 3 pounds. It is about the size of a big grapefruit.

Your cortex is the part of your brain that does most of your thinking. It receives messages from your eyes, ears, nose, tongue, and skin. It saves memories and makes decisions. It also helps to control your muscles.

Your cerebrum is divided into two halves that look like the halves of a walnut. The left half of your cerebrum controls the muscles of the right side of your body. And the right half of your cerebrum controls the muscles of the left side of your body.

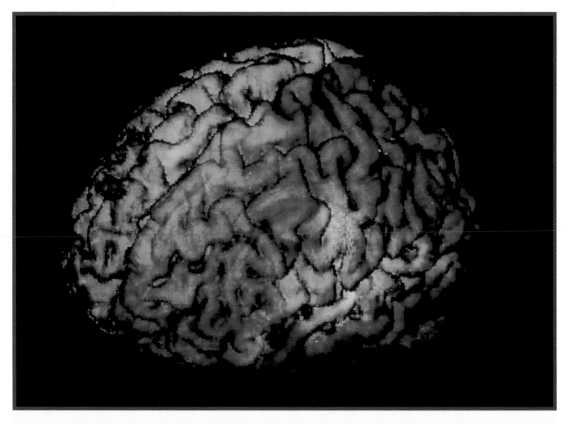

The bright areas in this picture are the parts of the cerebrum that help a person talk.

The right half of your brain helps you make music.

Each half of your cerebrum is good at doing different things. The left half is best at talking, reading, and doing math problems. The right half is best at making music and art, understanding shapes, imagining, and making jokes.

CHAPTER 5

WORKING TOGETHER

The parts of your nervous system work together. How do messages travel through your nervous system?

Your nerves, spinal cord, and brain work together. By working together, they keep your body running well.

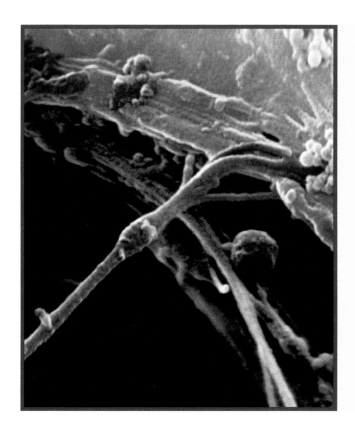

Nerve cells connect to one another to send messages through the body.

Your body collects millions of messages every day. Your nervous system ignores most of them. But every so often, a receptor collects an important message. Then the receptor passes the message on to a nerve. The nerve passes the message to your spinal cord. And your spinal cord passes it on to your brain. Your brain decides what to do about it.

Suppose receptors in your nose pick up a message. It's an interesting message. Your nerves carry the message to your brain. Your cerebrum goes through all of its smell memories. Aha! The message means that cookies are baking! Your cerebrum remembers that cookies are good to eat. It decides that you should go and get one.

When your nose smells freshly baked cookies, your nervous system sends a message to your brain.

Your brain knows what the smell of cookies means. It's time for a treat!

Your cerebellum takes over. It figures out how you need to move to go to the kitchen. Moments after your nose smelled the cookies, you are eating one.

All of this happens quickly. But sometimes there's an emergency. Your body needs to act even more quickly to keep you from being hurt. Then your spinal cord comes to the rescue.

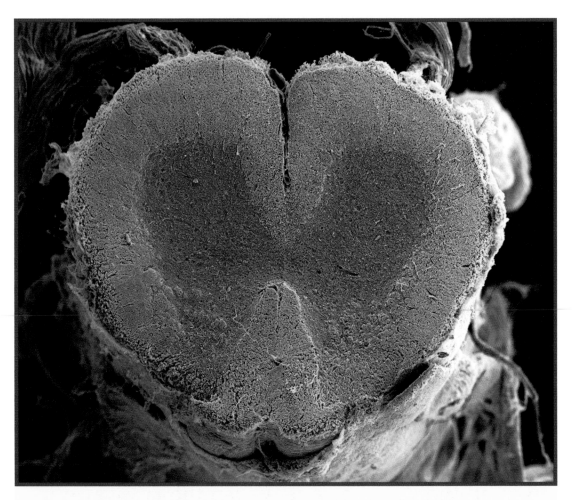

The nerve cells in your spinal cord work quickly. They help to keep you from being hurt.

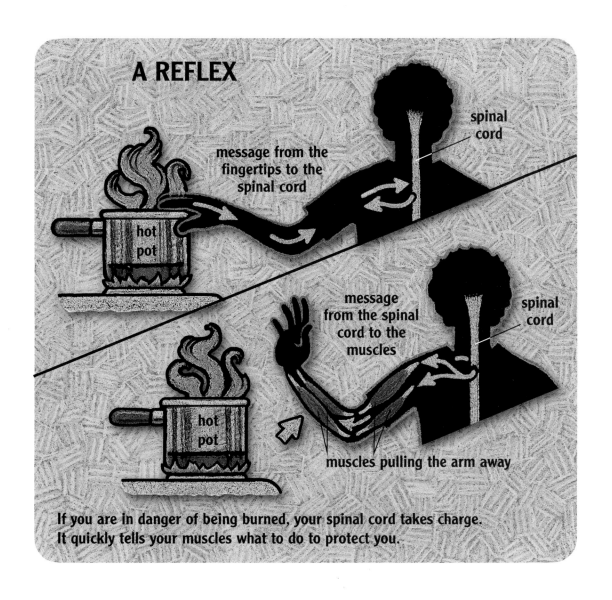

A REFLEX

message from the fingertips to the spinal cord

spinal cord

hot pot

message from the spinal cord to the muscles

spinal cord

hot pot

muscles pulling the arm away

If you are in danger of being burned, your spinal cord takes charge. It quickly tells your muscles what to do to protect you.

Your spinal cord helps to protect you by causing reflexes (REE-flehks-uhz). A reflex is something your body does even though you didn't think about doing it.

If you touch a hot pot, nerves in your skin send an emergency message. The message travels to your spinal cord. There is no time to send a message to your brain and ask it what to do. So your spinal cord causes a reflex. It sends a message to your arm muscles.

Touching something that is very hot can cause a bad burn.

If you touch a hot pot, your spinal cord makes you pull your hand away fast!

The message tells your muscles to pull your hand away from the pot. The muscles tighten, and your hand jerks away from the pot. The message travels so quickly that your hand pulls away before you even feel the heat! The spinal cord's fast action helps to keep you from being badly burned.

Your nervous system controls everything you do. It keeps your body running smoothly. It helps you remember where you live. It helps you throw a ball. It helps you decide what is right and what is wrong.

Your nervous system helps you hold and throw a ball.

Your nervous system helps you taste ice cream.

Your nervous system helps you make up stories and eat ice cream. It helps you laugh. Your nervous system makes you different from everyone else in the world. It makes you special.

ON SHARING A BOOK

When you share a book with a child, you show that reading is important. To get the most out of the experience, read in a comfortable, quiet place. Turn off the television and limit other distractions, such as telephone calls. Be prepared to start slowly. Take turns reading parts of this book. Stop occasionally and discuss what you're reading. Talk about the photographs. If the child begins to lose interest, stop reading. When you pick up the book again, revisit the parts you have already read.

BE A VOCABULARY DETECTIVE

The word list on page 5 contains words that are important in understanding the topic of this book. Be word detectives and search for the words as you read the book together. Talk about what the words mean and how they are used in the sentence. Do any of these words have more than one meaning? You will find the words defined in a glossary on page 46.

WHAT ABOUT QUESTIONS?

Use questions to make sure the child understands the information in this book. Here are some suggestions:

What did this paragraph tell us? What does this picture show? What do you think we'll learn about next? Why do you need nerves? How does your spinal cord help keep you safe? What does the brain stem do? What is your favorite part of the book? Why?

If the child has questions, don't hesitate to respond with questions of your own, such as: What do you think? Why? What is it that you don't know? If the child can't remember certain facts, turn to the index.

INTRODUCING THE INDEX

The index helps readers find information without searching through the whole book. Turn to the index on page 48. Choose an entry such as *nerves* and ask the child to use the index to find out what nerves are made of. Repeat with as many entries as you like. Ask the child to point out the differences between an index and a glossary. (The index helps readers find information, while the glossary tells readers what words mean.)

THE NERVOUS SYSTEM

BOOKS

Ballard, Carol. *How Do We Think?* Austin, TX: Raintree Steck-Vaughn, 1998. This book includes basic information about the brain along with activities to try.

Funston, Sylvia, and Jay Ingram. *It's All in Your Brain.* New York: Grosset & Dunlap, 1994. This exploratory trip through the brain covers the five senses—touch, taste, smell, sight, and sound.

Rowan, Peter. *Big Head!* New York: Knopf, 1998. Life-size illustrations and transparent pages show the inside and the outside of the head.

Silverstein, Alvin, and Virginia and Robert Silverstein. *The Nervous System.* New York: Twenty-First Century Books, 1994. This in-depth book covers all parts of the nervous system.

Swanson, Diane. *Hmm?: The Most Interesting Book You'll Ever Read About Memory.* Toronto: Kids Can Press, 2001. This book is packed with trivia, funny facts, and color illustrations.

WEBSITES

My Body
  http://www.kidshealth.org/kid/body/mybody.html
  This fun website has information on the systems of the human body, plus movies, games, and activities.

Neuroscience for Kids
  http://faculty.washington.edu/chudler/neurok.html
  This page includes facts about the brain and nervous system, along with experiments, activities, and links to other web pages.

Pathfinders for Kids: The Nervous System—The Control Center
  http://infozone.imcpl.org/kids_nerv.htm
  This web page has a list of resources you can use to learn more about the nervous system.

GLOSSARY

brain: the organ that keeps track of everything in the body

brain stem: the part of the brain that controls things the body does on its own

cerebellum (SAIR-uh-BEHL-uhm): the part of the brain that controls how the body moves

cerebrum (suh-REE-bruhm): the biggest part of the brain. It is divided into two halves. Each half is good at different things.

cortex: the wrinkly layer on the outside of the brain. It is the part of the brain that thinks, saves memories, and makes decisions.

nerves: bundles of cells that carry messages around the body

organs: parts of the body that do particular jobs. The brain, lungs, stomach, and heart are organs.

receptors (rih-SEHP-turz): nerve cells that collect information from the world and the body

reflexes (REE-flehks-uhz): something the body does automatically, without thinking about it

skull: the hard bones in the head that protect the brain

spinal cord: a bundle of nerve cells that runs through the backbone. It connects nerves to the brain.

INDEX

Pages listed in **bold** type refer to photographs.